CUBA

By Jagger Youssef and
Laura L. Sullivan

EXPLORING WORLD CULTURES

Cavendish Square

Published in 2027 by Cavendish Square Publishing, LLC
2544 Clinton Street, Buffalo, NY 14224

Second Edition

Website: cavendishsq.com

Library of Congress Cataloging-in-Publication Data

Names: Youssef, Jagger author | Sullivan, Laura L., 1974- author
Title: Cuba / Jagger Youssef and Laura L. Sullivan.
Description: New York : Cavendish Square Publishing, [2027] | Series: Exploring World Cultures | Includes index.
Identifiers: LCCN 2026004133 (print) | LCCN 2026004134 (ebook) | ISBN 9781502676993 library binding | ISBN 9781502676986 paperback | ISBN 9781502677006 ebook
Subjects: LCSH: Cuba
Classification: LCC F1758.5 .Y68 2027 (print) | LCC F1758.5 (ebook) | DDC 972.91--dc23/eng/20260218
LC record available at https://lccn.loc.gov/2026004133
LC ebook record available at https://lccn.loc.gov/2026004134

Writers: Jagger Youssef; Laura L. Sullivan (second edition)
Editor: Therese Shea
Designer: Deanna Lepovich

The photographs in this book are used by permission and through the courtesy of: Cover livcool/Shutterstock.com; p. 4 Image Source Limited/Alamy Photos; p. 5 Luciano Leon/Alamy Photos; p. 6 Sarfaraz82/Shutterstock.com; p. 7 imageBROKER.com/Alamy Photos; p. 8 Photo 12/Alamy Photos; p. 9 Fidel Castro (c. 1959)/Wikimedia Commons; p. 10 Liz Roll/Alamy Photos; p. 11 SOPA Images Limited/Alamy Photos; p. 12 Maciej Bledowski/Alamy Photos; p. 13 Michele Burgess/Alamy Photos; p. 14 Gabbro/Alamy Photos; p. 15 SantaClaraT/Alamy Photos; p. 16 Jo Crebbin/Alamy Photos; p. 17 courtesy of the Library of Congress; p. 18 Pascal Mannaerts/Alamy Photos; p. 19 Thiago Trevisan/Alamy Photos; p. 20 Jorge Royan/Alamy Photos; p. 21 robertharding/Alamy Photos; p. 22 Constantin Meehan/Shutterstock.com; p. 23 Kamira/Shutterstock.com; p. 24 Rosen Ivanov Iliev/Shutterstock.com; p. 25 Roberto Fumagalli/Alamy Photos; p. 27 (top) Imageplotter Travel/Alamy Photos; p. 27 (bottom) Bisual Photo/Shutterstock.com; p. 28 unpetitgraindefolie/Shutterstock.com; p. 29 Elena Eryomenko/Shutterstock.com

CPSIA compliance information: Batch #CS27CSQ: For further information contact Cavendish Square Publishing LLC at 1-877-980-4450.

Printed in United States of America

CONTENTS

Introduction 4

Chapter 1 Geography 6

Chapter 2 History 8

Chapter 3 Government 10

Chapter 4 The Economy 12

Chapter 5 The Environment 14

Chapter 6 The People Today 16

Chapter 7 Lifestyle 18

Chapter 8 Religion 20

Chapter 9 Language 22

Chapter 10 Arts and Festivals 24

Chapter 11 Fun and Play 26

Chapter 12 Food 28

Glossary 30

Find Out More 31

Index 32

INTRODUCTION

Cuba is a country in the Caribbean Sea. It's made up of many islands. The people of Cuba have mainly Native American, European, and African roots. Some are **descended** from other peoples too.

Cuba has a socialist government. This kind of government is one in which the government owns most businesses. Wealth is supposed to be spread evenly among citizens. However, Cuba has many problems, such as food shortages. Sometimes citizens aren't treated fairly. Many Cubans have moved to find a better life.

Cuba is called an island nation. It's more than one island, though.

Still, Cuba is a colorful country with friendly and hardworking people. In cities such as Havana, music and dancing happen every night. Cubans make tasty foods too.

People like to visit Cuba to enjoy its beautiful beaches. They learn a lot about Cuban **culture** by talking to the people who live there. It's not always easy for outsiders to travel to Cuba, though. If you can't get to Cuba, reading about it is the next best thing.

If you're in Cuba, you're never far from the beach!

GEOGRAPHY

On a map, you can find Cuba south of the United States. Cuba is where three large bodies of water meet: the Caribbean Sea, the Atlantic Ocean, and the Gulf of Mexico (called the Gulf of America by some).

The capital city of Cuba is Havana. It's also the biggest city on the main island. Most of Cuba is low and flat, with small hills. There are some mountains in the southeast. Pico Turquino is the highest point, at 6,476 feet (1,974 meters). The Cauto is the longest of Cuba's major rivers.

FACT!

The entire country of Cuba has more than 4,000 islands! Most are very small.

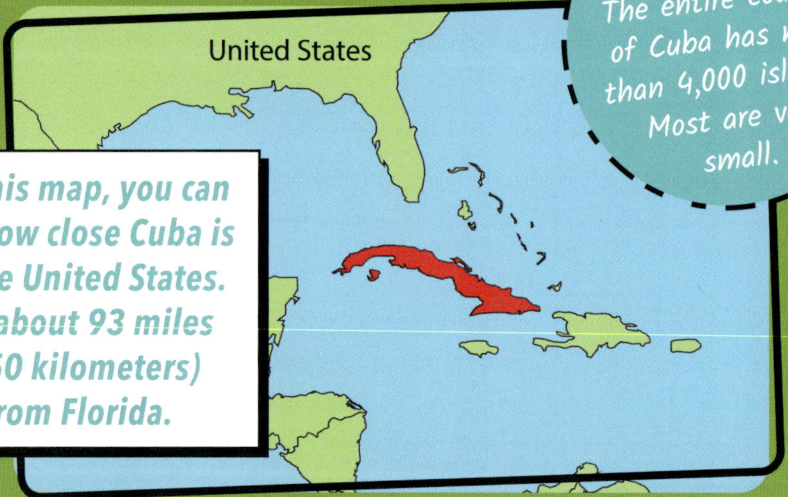

On this map, you can see how close Cuba is to the United States. It's about 93 miles (150 kilometers) from Florida.

Cuba's climate is tropical. It's always warm and often wet. Its dry season is from November to April, and its rainy season is from May to October. **Hurricanes** bring strong winds and flooding during the rainy season.

Cuba has more than 3,500 miles (5,630 km) of coastline.

MEASURING CUBA

The main island of Cuba is long and narrow. It's about 120 miles (190 km) across at its widest point. It's 19 miles (30 km) across at its narrowest point. Cuba is about 777 miles (1,250 km) long. It's the largest Caribbean island.

HISTORY

The Taíno people lived on Cuba since about 500 CE. Italian explorer Christopher Columbus came to Cuba in 1492. He claimed the land for Spain. The Spanish **enslaved** the Taíno. They passed on European sicknesses too. Many Taíno died.

Cuba was ruled by Spain until 1898. It then became an independent, or free, country. In 1959, after a **revolution**, Fidel Castro took control. He wanted a **communist** nation, in which the government owned the land, farms, and factories, and workers received what they needed to live. In real life, Cuba's government often didn't provide enough for citizens to live.

José Martí was a Cuban national hero who helped lead Cuba's fight for independence from Spain in the late 1800s.

Fidel Castro led Cuba for 49 years.

In 2019, the Cuban people approved a new constitution, or set of laws. It limits a president's time in office. The constitution included new rights for citizens too.

FACT!

The English language uses some Taíno words, including barbecue, potato, and iguana.

CUBAN MISSILE CRISIS

In 1962, the Soviet Union, another communist nation, placed **missiles** on Cuba. The United States feared war and asked for them to be removed. The two countries came to an agreement, and the missiles were taken away.

GOVERNMENT

Cuba's official name is the Republic of Cuba. The Communist Party is the only group allowed to take part in the government. The government has three parts: executive, legislative, and judicial.

The first secretary of the Communist Party has the most power. Below them is the president. Cuba's new constitution added the position of prime minister. This spreads power more evenly within the executive branch.

President Raúl Castro allowed Cubans to have cell phones and computers for the first time.

Miguel Díaz-Canel Bermúdez, left, promised more freedoms to Cubans. He remained loyal to the Communist Party's ideas, though.

FACT!
In Cuba, all people 16 and older can vote.

The legislative branch makes the laws. It includes the Council of State and the National Assembly of People's Power.

The judicial branch is made up of courts. The highest court is the People's Supreme Court.

In today's Cuba, the people can own more property, businesses, and farms. However, the government still controls and limits people's freedoms.

CHANGE IN LEADERSHIP

In 2008, Raúl Castro, Fidel's brother, became president. Miguel Díaz-Canel Bermúdez became president of Cuba in 2019. He has been first secretary of the Communist Party since 2021.

THE ECONOMY

Cuba's **economy** remains largely controlled by the government. The government owns most of the factories and farms and employs most of the workers. Since the 1990s, the government has allowed more people to own companies and farms. As of 2025, about 40 percent of Cubans work for privately owned companies and farms.

FACT!

Cuba often has shortages of certain foods, medicines, and goods.

In 2026, one Cuban peso was worth about 42 U.S. cents.

Cuban money is called the peso. The Cuban peso is used to pay workers and to buy most things. The government gives Cuban citizens a **ration** book, or *libreta*, to get basic foods such as sugar, rice, or cooking oil.

Cuba sells goods such as sugar, fruit, coffee, tobacco, and fish to other countries. More people are traveling to Cuba to visit too. About 1.8 million people visited the island in 2025.

Cuba has many wonderful markets to buy food and other goods.

TRADE

By law, the United States does very little trade with Cuba. However, Cuba buys American food and medicines, or drugs that help sick people. The United States buys Cuban art and a few other things.

THE ENVIRONMENT

Cuba has thousands of different plants and animals. Some only live in this nation. Palm trees and orchids are examples of plants. Cork palm trees are some of the rarest trees in the world.

Birds such as flamingos and nightingales live near the rivers. Tortoises and many kinds of frogs live there too. Manatees live along the coast. Rare Cuban crocodiles live in the Zapata Swamp. Cuban rock iguanas climb trees.

FACT!

*Cuba's largest land animal is a **rodent** called the hutia. It can weigh as much as 20 pounds (9 kilograms)!*

The trogon (or tocororo) is the national bird of Cuba.

The Cuban **environment** has some troubles. Many forests have been cut down. Unclean air is another problem. Since the 1980s, the government has tried to help the environment more. In 2017, the Cuban government passed a special plan called Tarea Vida (Life Task).

Cuba's national flower is the white mariposa.

TAREA VIDA

Cuba's normal patterns of weather, or its climate, are changing. The government's Tarea Vida plan aims to help the country deal with the changes.

THE PEOPLE TODAY

Because of Cuba's history, many people have a Native American, European, or African background. People from different backgrounds often marry each other. As of 2023, about 10 million people lived in Cuba. More than 2 million lived in the city of Havana.

FACT!

According to U.S. law, Americans aren't allowed to spend money at businesses or other places owned by the Cuban government.

Cubans may wear special clothing for visitors and special events.

After the Communist Revolution, a lot of Cubans went to the United States. People in Cuba couldn't visit their family members who moved there. Today, it's still hard to travel between these two countries. However, Americans can go for certain reasons, such as to aid Cuban people and to help privately owned businesses.

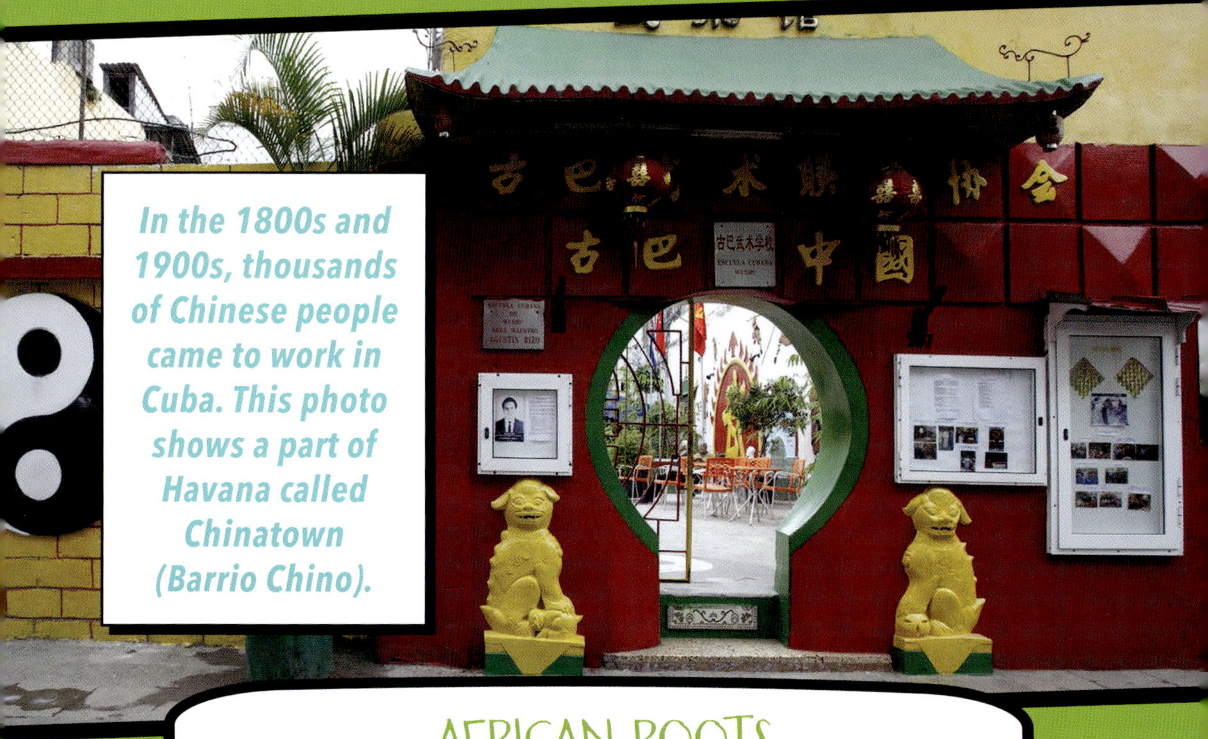

In the 1800s and 1900s, thousands of Chinese people came to work in Cuba. This photo shows a part of Havana called Chinatown (Barrio Chino).

AFRICAN ROOTS

Enslaved Africans worked on Cuban sugar farms beginning in the 1500s. Slavery was outlawed in 1886. Some Cubans today have African roots because of this history.

LIFESTYLE

Cuban people are friendly and welcoming. The law says women are equal to men in government and at work. It also says they have to be treated equally at home. However, most women are still expected to cook, clean, and take care of children. Many Cuban women decide to not have children because of hardship in their lives.

Playing dominoes is one of the most popular ways to spend time with others in Cuba.

Cubans spend a lot of time outdoors.

FACT!

In 2023, Cuban women held more than half of the seats in the National Assembly of People's Power.

Cuban children must attend school from ages six to sixteen. Students then have to pass tests to get into college. Young men also need to spend two years in the armed forces. School in Cuba is free. It's paid for by the government. Nearly all Cubans can read.

BETTER TOGETHER

When Cuban people aren't working, they spend time with their family and friends. They take walks together, drink coffee, and play games.

RELIGION

Most Cubans practice a **religion**. Christians make up the largest group, especially Catholics. Smaller groups practice religions such as Hinduism, Buddhism, Islam, and Judaism.

Santería is a common religion in Cuba. Enslaved Africans brought their beliefs to Cuba and these beliefs mixed with Catholicism. Santería is also called Regla de Ocha (Rule of Ocha). "Ocha" is the word for gods. Some people attend both Catholic and Santería services.

Many Cubans ask Santería leaders for advice and sometimes healing.

Cubans didn't have religious freedom after the Communist Revolution. Religious people couldn't join the Communist Party. After 1992, the constitution changed to protect people with religious beliefs more. More people practice a religion today. However, about one-fifth of Cubans practice no religion.

CASTRO VS. THE CHURCH

Fidel Castro and the communist revolutionaries saw religious people as enemies. However, the government soon understood that religions could help Cubans, such as providing food and goods to live. So, Cuba allowed some religious freedom.

FACT!
About half of all Cubans are Roman Catholic.

Havana Cathedral once held the remains of Christopher Columbus.

LANGUAGE

The official language of Cuba is Spanish. Some Spanish words are said differently in Cuba than in other countries that speak Spanish. So, the language is sometimes called Cuban Spanish, or Cubano.

Cuban Spanish borrows words from other languages. Some words come from the native Taíno people. English words are used too. They're a bit different though. For example, Cubans say *chopi* for "shopping."

FACT!
Cuban Spanish is spoken differently in different parts of Cuba.

"Havana" is the common English spelling for the capital of Cuba. "Habana" is the Spanish name.

Greetings can be either more polite or more relaxed. People use relaxed language with family members and close friends. Polite language is used with older people or strangers. Usually, it's okay to use relaxed words with everyone.

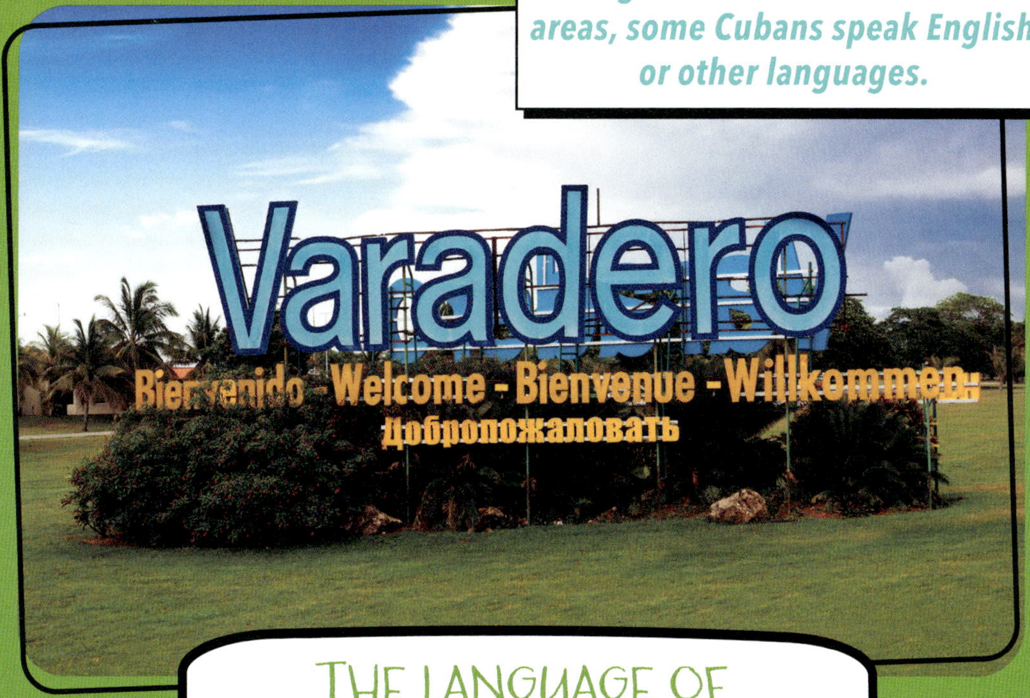

In larger Cuban cities and tourist areas, some Cubans speak English or other languages.

THE LANGUAGE OF COMMUNISM

Many Cubans began to say *compañero* or *compañera* ("comrade" or "friend") after the Communist Revolution. They still say it today. It's meant to show equality among people.

ARTS AND FESTIVALS

Art in Cuba comes from the Cuban people's lives and history. Some Cuban artists and musicians celebrate Cuba. Others paint, draw, or sing to ask for change in their country.

Cuban music blends Spanish and African music. Popular forms of music are son cubano, habanera, mambo, bolero, rumba, and cha-cha. Many of these styles have their own dance steps too.

FACT!

Afro-Cuban jazz is the early form of Latin jazz, which is popular all over the world.

Street art is becoming common in Cuba. It's a way for people to spread their ideas.

The Cuban National Ballet School is the biggest in the world. About 3,000 dancers study there.

Cuba has many festivals, or celebrations, during the year. There are jazz festivals, film festivals, and book fairs. On May 1, Cubans celebrate their country, its workers, and socialism. A similar holiday is the Santiago de Cuba Carnival. It's the biggest carnival in Cuba and held from July 18 to July 27. It celebrates the Communist Revolution. It also celebrates people's backgrounds and culture.

SON CUBANO

Son cubano (Cuban sound) is a kind of Cuban music and dance. It blends Spanish guitar, singing, and African beats.

FUN AND PLAY

In Cuba, sports are a part of everyday life. Children must learn baseball, volleyball, basketball, gymnastics, and track and field in school. Many Cubans continue to play sports as adults.

Baseball is Cuba's national sport. More than half of all Cubans play baseball. When kids get together, it's often to play baseball. Basketball is popular too. The Cuban national basketball team is the only Caribbean basketball team to win a medal at the Olympics as of 2025. Boxing and volleyball are popular in Cuba too.

Cubans also enjoy water activities such as swimming, sailing, paddleboarding, snorkeling, and scuba diving.

MEDAL WINNERS

Cuba won the first Olympic gold medal for baseball, at the 1992 Olympics. Cuban teams have won medals in five of the six Olympics in which baseball was played.

The top sport in most Caribbean nations is soccer. But in Cuba, baseball is the top sport.

FACT!

The Cuban men's national basketball team won the bronze medal at the 1972 Munich Olympics.

It's not uncommon for Cuban children to make their own ball when playing soccer or another sport.

FOOD

Cuban food is a tasty blend of cultures. Over the years, the dishes of Spanish, African, and Taíno peoples have become the food of Cuba. Most meals include rice and beans. If served side by side, this is called *arroz con frijoles* (rice with beans). Chicken and beef may be served with them. Fresh seafood is also widely eaten in most places.

The Cuban coffee drink called café cubano is both strong and sweet.

CUBAN DESSERTS

Cuban desserts are often very sweet. Flan is a caramel custard. Tres leches cake is a creamy sponge cake. Arroz con leche is a sugary rice pudding. Pastelitos are pastries with sweet fillings.

The famous toasted Cuban sandwich has roasted pork, ham, Swiss cheese, mustard, and pickles between buttered bread. Cubans have many tasty snacks such as crispy, fried **plantains** called *tostones*.

Cuban fruits are made into drinks such as guava juice and mango nectar. Dining at a Cuban restaurant is a great way to get to know Cuban culture.

FACT!
Cuba's national dish is ropa vieja. This is beef in a tomato sauce with vegetables.

Cuban foods, such as the ropa vieja shown here, are usually flavorful but not spicy.

GLOSSARY

communist: A kind of government and economy in which individuals don't own land, factories, or machinery, the government or community do. Everyone is supposed to share wealth.

culture: The beliefs and ways of life of a group of people.

descend: To come after another in a family.

economy: The money made in an area and how it is made.

enslaved: To be forced to work without pay under terrible conditions.

environment: The natural world in which a plant or animal lives.

hurricane: A powerful storm that forms over water and causes heavy rainfall and high winds.

missile: A rocket used to strike something at a distance.

plaintain: A tropical fruit similar to a banana with green skin.

ration: A fixed amount of food people are allowed during a time of shortage.

religion: A belief in and way of honoring a god or gods.

revolution: A movement to overthrow an established government.

rodent: A small, furry animal with large front teeth, such as a mouse or rat.

FIND OUT MORE

Books

Anderson, Shannon. *Cuba*. Minneapolis, MN: Bellwether Media, 2024.

Klepeis, Alicia. *Cuba*. Mendota Heights, MN: Focus Readers, 2025.

Websites

Cuba
kids.nationalgeographic.com/geography/countries/article/cuba
Read a great review of the nation and its culture from National Geographic Kids.

Video

Exploring Cuba
socialstudiesonline.com/exploring-cuba-video/
This video provides more history and culture of the island nation.

Publisher's note to educators and parents: Our editors have carefully reviewed these websites to ensure that they are suitable for students. Many websites change frequently, however, and we cannot guarantee that a site's future contents will continue to meet our high standards of quality and educational value. Be advised that students should be closely supervised whenever they access the internet.

INDEX

A

African, 4, 16, 17, 20, 24, 25
26, 28
Atlantic Ocean, 6

B

baseball, 26, 27
basketball, 26, 27
Bermúdez, Miguel Díaz-
Canel, 11

C

Caribbean Sea, 4, 6
Castro, Fidel, 8, 9, 11, 21
Castro, Raúl, 10, 11
Catholicism, 20, 21
Chinese, 17
Columbus, Christopher, 8, 21
communism, 8, 9, 17, 21, 23,
25
Communist Party, 10, 11, 21
constitution, 9, 10, 21

F

first secretary of the
Communist Party, 10, 11

H

Havana, 5, 6, 16, 17, 21, 22

M

Martí ,José, 8
music, 5, 24, 25

O

Olympics, 26, 27

P

prime minister, 10

R

ration books, 13

S

Santería, 20
schools, 19, 25, 26
Spain, 8, 9
Spanish, 8, 22, 24, 25, 28

T

Taíno, 8, 9, 22, 28